The Motivational
Book of Quotes:

500+ Motivational Quotes
for Increased Positivity,
Confidence and Success

The Motivational Book of Quotes: 500 Motivational Quotes for Increased Positivity, Confidence and Motivation

Copyright © 2017 by Jenny Kellett

Cover by: Jenny Kellett

ISBN-13: 978-1976399954
ISBN-10: 1976399955

Give feedback on the book at:
me@jennykellett.com

Printed in U.S.A

Introduction

No one said the road to success was easy — there are always pitfalls along the way, and procrastination is one of the biggest productivity killers.

Even the most motivated of people have days when they struggle to get out of bed or keep working on the goals they have set. Sometimes even the best of us need a push in the right direction to get started.

Often all it takes to get back on track is to be inspired by others that have achieved success in their own lives and are passing on their wisdom to you.

Whether you're running your own business or simply want to be inspired to be a better person, inspirational and motivational quotes are a simple way to get that kick start.

Not every quote in this book will resonate with everyone, but when you find the one that just 'clicks' with you, write it down and remember it. Put it up on your wall or write it on a Post-It and stick it on your computer to look at when you're having a lapse in productivity.

Here's to a productive and successful future!

My favorite quotes...

Don't watch the clock; do what it does.
Keep going.

— Sam Levenson

///////////

It's not about perfect. It's about effort. And
when you bring that effort every single day,
that's where transformation happens. That's
how change occurs.

— Jillian Michaels

///////////

A river cuts through rock, not because of its
power but because of its persistence.

— Jim Watkins

Wherever you are, be all there.

— *Jim Elliot*

////////

If it doesn't challenge you, it doesn't change you.

— *Fred DeVito*

////////

Believe in yourself! Have faith in your abilities! Without a humble but reasonable confidence in your own powers you cannot be successful or happy.

— *Norman Vincent Peale*

Ever tried. Ever failed. No matter. Try Again. Fail again. Fail better.

— *Samuel Beckett*

//////////

Be so good they can't ignore you.

— *Steve Martin*

//////////

You are never too old to set another goal or to dream another dream.

— *Les Brown*

It is better to live for one day as a lion than for 1000 days as a sheep.

— *Tibetan proverb*

///////////

You can't have a better tomorrow if you're still thinking about yesterday.

— *Charles F. Kettering*

///////////

When you fail you learn from the mistakes you made and it motivates you to work even harder.

— *Natalie Gulbis*

Perfection is not attainable, but if we chase perfection we can catch excellence.

— *Vince Lombardi*

////////

It is better to fail in originality than to succeed in imitation.

— *Herman Melville*

////////

If you don't value your time, neither will others. Stop giving away your time and talents- start charging for it.

— *Kim Garst*

Don't fight the problem, decide it.

— *George C. Marshall*

////////

When one must, one can.

— *Charlotte Whitton*

////////

Set your goals high and don't stop until you get there.

— *Bo Jackson*

Work hard in silence, let your success be your noise.

— Frank Ocean

//////////

Don't stop when you're tired, stop when you're done.

— Unknown

//////////

Push yourself because no one else is going to do it for you.

— Unknown

It always seems impossible until it's done.

— Nelson Mandela

//////////

Make up your mind that no matter what comes your way, no matter how difficult, no matter how unfair, you will do more than simply survive. You will thrive in spite of it.

— Joel Osteen

//////////

Mistakes are the portals of discovery.

— James Joyce

You can't expect to hit the jackpot if you don't put a few nickels in the machine.

—Flip Wilson

////////

You are never given a wish without also being given the power to make it come true. You may have to work for it, however.

— Richard David Bach

////////

Never retreat. Never explain. Get it done and let them howl.

— Benjamin Jowett

Be gentle to all and stern with yourself.

— *Saint Teresa of Avila*

/////////

You may only succeed if you desire succeeding; you may only fail if you do not mind failing.

— *Philippos*

/////////

March on. Do not tarry. To go forward is to move toward perfection. March on, and fear not the thorns, or the sharp stones on life's path.

— *Khalil Gibran*

No bird soars too high if he soars with his own wings.

— William Blake

///////////

The secret of getting ahead is getting started.

— Mark Twain

///////////

Expect problems and eat them for breakfast.

— Alfred A. Montapert

Collect moments, not things.

— Unknown

///////////

Put your heart, mind and soul into even your smallest acts. This is the secret of success.

— Swami Sivananda

///////////

All progress takes place outside the comfort zone.

— Michael John Bobak

All our dreams can come true if we have the courage to pursue them.

— *Walt Disney*

///////////

You can't start the next chapter of your life if you keep re-reading the last one.

— *Unknown*

///////////

Where there is a will, there is a way. If there is a chance in a million that you can do something, anything, to keep what you want from ending, do it. Pry the door open or, if need be, wedge your foot in that door and keep it open.

— Pauline Keal

////////

Start by doing what's necessary; then do what's possible; and suddenly you are doing the impossible.

— Francis of Assissi

////////

Don't think, just do. — Horace
There is progress whether ye are going forward or backward! The thing is to move!

— Edgar Cayce

Go big or go home. Because it's true. What do you have to lose?

— *Eliza Dushku*

////////////

Pursue one great decisive aim with force and determination.

— *Carl von Clausewitz*

////////////

You can't build a reputation on what you are going to do.

— *Henry Ford*

Leap, and the net will appear.

— *John Burroughs*

//////////

Some people dream of success, while other people get up every morning and make it happen.

— *Wayne Huizenga*

//////////

What you do today can improve all your tomorrows.

— *Ralph Marston*

Just believe in yourself. Even if you don't, pretend that you do and, at some point, you will.

— *Venus Williams*

///////

The best motivation for tomorrow is doing your best today.

— *H. Jackson Brown, Jr.*

///////

Crave for a thing, you will get it. Renounce the craving, the object will follow you by itself.

— *Swami Sivananda*

Good words bring good feelings to the heart. Speak with kindness, always.

— Fred Williams

////////

To accomplish great things, we must not only act, but also dream, not only plan, but also believe.

— Anatole France

////////

Push harder than yesterday if you want a different tomorrow.

— Unknown

In life, we are all on our separate paths. Sometimes our paths will cross, sometimes we will have to take a longer way round. Ultimately though, we all have a final destination and getting there is called living.

— *Nicolas Attwood*

///////////

Keep your eyes on the stars, and your feet on the ground.

— *Theodore Roosevelt*

In the face of such hopelessness as our eventual, unavoidable death, there is little sense in not at least trying to accomplish all of your wildest dreams in life.

— *Kevin Smith*

////////

Some of the best lessons we ever learn are learned from past mistakes. The error of the past is the wisdom and success of the future.

— *Dale Turner*

People who are crazy enough to think they can change the world, are the ones who do.

— *Rob Siltanen*

////////

Only put off until tomorrow what you are willing to die having left undone.

— *Pablo Picasso*

////////

Success isn't always about greatness. It's about consistency. Consistent hard work leads to success. Greatness will come.

— *Dwayne Johnson*

Success is not a good teacher, failure
makes you humble.

— Shah Rukh Khan

////////

A creative man is motivated by the desire
to achieve, not by the desire to beat others.

— Ayn Rand

////////

Courage is resistance to fear, mastery of
fear - not absence of fear.

— Mark Twain

Just when the caterpillar thought the world was ending, he turned into a butterfly.

— *Proverb*

////////

Little minds are tamed and subdued by misfortune; but great minds rise above it.

— *Washington Irving*

////////

People often say that motivation doesn't last. Well, neither does bathing - that's why we recommend it daily.

— *Zig Ziglar*

Purpose is the best alarm clock ever.

— *Jordan Chenery*

///////////

Difficult roads often lead to beautiful destinations.

— *Unknown*

///////////

Be very strong. Be very methodical in your life if you want to be a champion.

— *Alberto Juantorena*

Innovation distinguishes between a leader and a follower.

— *Steve Jobs*

////////////

Many are called, but few get up.

— *Oliver Herford*

////////////

Only the educated are free.

— *Epictetus*

Be thine own palace, or the world's thy jail.

— John Donne

///////////

Victory belongs to the most persevering.

— Napoleon Bonaparte

///////////

The pessimist sees difficulty in every opportunity. The optimist sees the opportunity in every difficulty.

— Winston Churchill

Education breeds confidence.

— Confucius

///////////

You measure the size of the
accomplishment by the obstacles you had
to overcome to reach your goals.

— Booker T. Washington

///////////

The best and most beautiful things in the
world cannot be seen or even touched —
they must be felt with the heart.

— Helen Keller

We may encounter many defeats but we must not be defeated.

— *Maya Angelou*

////////

Beginning today, treat everyone you meet as if they were going to be dead by midnight. Extend to them all the care, kindness and understand you can muster, and do it with no thought of any reward. Your life will never be the same again.

— *Og Mandino*

No matter how you feel, get up, dress up, show up and never give up.

— *Unknown*

///////////

Strength and growth come only through continuous effort and struggle.

— *Napoleon Hill*

///////////

Winning isn't everything, but wanting it is.

— *Arnold Palmer*

Fortune sides with him who dares.

— *Virgil*

//////////

The world breaks everyone, and afterward, some are strong at the broken places.

— *Ernest Hemingway*

//////////

You may have to fight a battle more than once to win it.

— *Margaret Thatcher*

From my tribe I take nothing, I am the maker of my own fortune.

— *Tecumseh*

////////

They tried to bury us. They didn't know they were seeds.

— *Mexican proverb*

////////

Never look to others to find motivation... look inside yourself

— *John Kellett*

Only dead fish go with the flow.

— *Unknown*

///////////

I'm not here to be average, I'm here to be awesome.

— *Unknown*

///////////

Live as if you were to die tomorrow. Learn as if you were to live forever.

— *Mahatma Gandhi*

Never give up on a dream just because of the time it will take to accomplish it. The time will pass anyway.

— *Earl Nightingale*

////////////

The future belongs to those that believe in the beauty of their dreams.

— *Eleanor Roosevelt*

////////////

We must let go of the life we have planned, so as to accept the one that is waiting for us.

— *Joseph Campbell*

Successful entrepreneurs are givers and not takers of positive energy.

— *Anonymous*

////////////

Set your sights high, the higher the better. Expect the most wonderful things to happen, not in the future but right now. Realize that nothing is too good. Allow absolutely nothing to hamper you, or hold you up in any way.

— *Eileen Caddy*

////////////

One finds limits by pushing them.

— *Herbert Simon*

A champion needs a motivation above and beyond winning.

— *Pat Riley*

////////

A year from now you will wish you had started today.

— *Karen Lamb*

////////

We cannot stay home all our lives, we must present ourselves to the world and we must look upon it as an adventure.

— *Beatrix Potter*

Hitch your wagon to a star.

— Ralph Waldo Emerson

///////////

You simply have to put one foot in front of the other and keep going. Put blinders on and plow right ahead.

— George Lucas

///////////

Success is...knowing your purpose in life, growing to reach your maximum potential, and sowing seeds that benefit others.

— John C. Maxwell

Every accomplishment starts with the decision to try.

— *Unknown*

////////

You just can't beat the person who never gives up.

— *Babe Ruth*

////////

Everybody is a genius. But if you judge a fish by its ability to climb a tree, it will live its whole life believing that it is stupid.

— *Albert Einstein*

Education is the most powerful weapon that you can use to change the world.

— *Nelson Mandela*

///////////

There will be obstacles. There will be doubters. There will be mistakes. But with hard work, there are no limits.

— *Michael Phelps*

///////////

Trust because you are willing to accept the risk, not because it's safe or certain.

— *Anonymous*

It's kind of fun to do the impossible.

— *Walt Disney*

////////

The greatest danger for most of us is not that our aim is too high and we miss it, but that it is too low and we reach it.

— *Michelangelo*

////////

You can't connect the dots looking forward; you can only connect them looking backwards. So you have to trust that the dots will somehow connect in your future. You have to trust in something - your gut, destiny, life, karma, whatever. This approach has never let me down, and it has made all the difference in my life.

— *Steve Jobs*

//////////

I've learned that people will forget what you said, but people will never forget how you made them feel.

— *Maya Angelou*

//////////

In my experience, there is only one motivation, and that is desire. No reasons or principle contain it or stand against it.

— *Jane Smiley*

Aim for the moon. If you miss, you may hit a star.

— *W. Clement Stone*

////////

Many of the things you can count, don't count. Many of the things you can't count, really count.

— *Albert Einstein*

////////

Things do not happen. Things are made to happen.

— *John F. Kennedy*

If you care about what you do and work hard at it, there isn't anything you can't do it you want to.

— Jim Henson

///////////

Good things come to people who wait, but better things come to those who go out and get them.

— Anonymous

///////////

I've found that luck is quite predictable. If you want more luck, take more chances. Be more active. Show up more often.

— Brian Tracy

The whole problem with the world is that fools and fanatics are always so certain of themselves, and wiser people so full of doubt.

— Bertrand Russell

////////

In the practice of tolerance, one's enemy is the best teacher.

— The Dalai Lama

////////

Opportunity is missed by most people because it is dressed in overalls and looks like work.

— Thomas Edison

Everybody can be great because anybody can serve.

— *Martin Luther King, Jr.*

////////

I've worked too hard and too long to let anything stand in the way of my goals. I will not let my teammates down and I will not let myself down.

— *Mia Hamm*

////////

Never give up, for that is just the place and time that the tide will turn.

— *Harriet Beecher Stowe*

Stay away from negative people. They have a problem for every solution.

— Albert Einstein

///////////

When you stop chasing the wrong things you give the right things a chance to catch you.

— Lolly Daskal

///////////

We come to love not by finding the perfect person, but by learning to see an imperfect person perfectly.

— Angelina Jolie

Love begins at home, and it is not how much we do... but how much love we put into that action.

— *Mother Teresa*

///////////

Success is no accident. It is hard work, perseverance, learning, studying, sacrifice and most of all, love of what you are doing or learning to do.

— *Pele*

///////////

To improve is to change; to be perfect is to change often.

— *Winston Churchill*

Don't chase people. Be yourself, do your own thing and work hard. The right people — the ones who really belong in your life — will come to you. And stay.

— *Will Smith*

////////

It is not what we take up but what we give up, that makes us rich.

— *Henry Ward Beecher*

////////

If you genuinely want something, don't wait for it — teach yourself to be impatient.

— *Gurbaksh Chahal*

Think little goals and expect little achievements. Think big goals and win big success.

— David Joseph Schwartz

////////

There are no secrets to success. It is the result of preparation, hard work, and learning from failure.

— Colin Powell

////////

If you don't ask, you don't get.

— Stevie Wonder

The number one reason people fail in life is because they listen to their friends, family, and neighbors.

— *Napoleon Hill*

//////////

Life is not measured by the number of breaths we take, but by the moments that take our breath away.

— *Maya Angelou*

//////////

To live is the rarest thing in the world. Most people just exist.

— *Oscar Wilde*

If you spend too much time thinking about a thing, you'll never get it done.

— *Bruce Lee*

////////

Success is how high you bounce when you hit the bottom.

— *George S. Patton*

////////

Millions of people can believe in you, and yet none of that matters if you don't believe in yourself.

— *Unknown*

Thinking should become your capital asset, no matter whatever ups and downs you come across in your life.

— *Dr APJ Kalam*

///////////

Don't worry about being successful but work toward being significant and the success will follow.

— *Oprah Winfrey*

///////////

It's not whether you get knocked down, it's whether you get back up.

— *Vince Lombardi*

People cry, not because they're weak. But because they've been strong for too long.

— *Johnny Depp*

////////

Your positive action combined with positive thinking results in success.

— *Shiv Kher*

////////

Set yourself earnestly to see what you are made to do, and then set yourself earnestly to do it.

— *Phillips Brooks*

Take up one idea. Make that one idea your life - think of it, dream of it, live on that idea. Let the brain, muscles, nerves, every part of your body, be full of that idea, and just leave every other idea alone. This is the way to success.

— *Swami Vivekananda*

////////////

Decide what you want, decide what you are willing to exchange for it. Establish your priorities and go to work.

— *H. L. Hunt*

The successful warrior is the average man, with laser-like focus.

— Bruce Lee

///////////

Do one thing every day that scares you.

— Anonymous

///////////

There's a way to do it better — find it.

— Thomas A. Edison

A goal is a dream with a deadline.

— Napoleon Hill

////////////

Be stronger than your excuse.

— Nike slogan

////////////

The price of greatness is responsibility.

— Sir Winston Churchill

Lots of people will ride with you in the limo, but what you want is someone who will take the bus with you when the limo breaks down.

— Oprah Winfrey

////////

All men should strive to learn before they die, what they are running from, and to, and why.

— James Thurber

////////

To live a creative life, we must lose our fear of being wrong.

— Anonymous

If you don't like how things are, change it. You are not a tree!

— *Jim Rohn*

////////

Problems are not stop signs, they are guidelines.

— *Robert H. Schuller*

////////

I believe there's an inner power that makes winners or losers. And the winners are the ones who listen to the truth of their hearts.

— *Sylvester Stallone*

Nowadays people know the price of everything and the value of nothing.

— *Oscar Wilde*

///////////

It is not only for what we do that we are held responsible, but also for what we do not do.

— *Moliere*

///////////

As you become more clear about who you really are, you'll be better able to decide what is best for you — the first time around.

— *Oprah Winfrey*

Be yourself. Everyone else is already taken.

— *Oscar Wilde*

//////////

If you want to live a happy life, tie it to a goal, not to people or objectives.

— *Albert Einstein*

//////////

I set out on a journey of love, seeking truth, peace and understanding. I am still learning.

— *Muhammad Ali*

You must do things you think you cannot do.

— Eleanor Roosevelt

////////////

Don't tell people your dreams. Show them.

— Unknown

////////////

Great minds discuss ideas. Average minds discuss events. Small minds discuss people.

— Eleanor Roosevelt

Seize the day. Because, believe it or not, each and every one of us in this room is one day going to stop breathing.

— *Robin Williams*

///////////

Opportunity doesn't knock, it presents itself when you beat down the door.

— *Kyle Chandler*

///////////

I am always doing that which I cannot do, in order that I may learn how to do it.

— *Pablo Picasso*

I haven't a clue how my story will end, but that's all right. When you set out on a journey and night covers the road, that's when you discover the stars.

— *Nancy Willard*

////////

Kites rise highest against the wind, not with it.

— *Sir Winston Churchill*

////////

Forgive yourself for your faults and your mistakes and move on.

— *Les Brown*

No matter how many goals you have achieved, you must set your sights on a higher one.

— *Jessica Savitch*

///////////

The people who influence you are the people who believe in you.

— *Henry Drummond*

///////////

I really believe that everyone has a talent, ability, or skill that he can mine to support himself and to succeed in life.

— *Dean Koontz*

Do your work with your whole heart,
and you will succeed – there's so little
competition.

– Elbert Hubbard

////////////

Consult not your fears, but your hopes and
your dreams.

– Pope John XXIII

////////////

Either move or be moved.

– Ezra Pound

The more things you do, the more things you can do.

— *Lucille Ball*

////////

Motivation is the art of getting people to do what you want them to do because they want to do it.

— *Dwight D. Eisenhower*

////////

Either I will find a way, or I will make one.

— *Philip Sidney*

Always desire to learn something useful.

— *Sophocles*

////////

The whole secret of a successful life is to find out what is one's destiny to do, and then do it.

— *Henry Ford*

////////

Never complain and never explain.

— *Benjamin Disraeli*

I attribute my success to this — I never gave or took an excuse.

— Florence Nightingale

///////////

The more man meditates upon good thoughts, the better will be his world and the world at large.

— Confucius

///////////

To be a good loser is to learn how to win.

— Carl Sandburg

I learned that we can do anything, but not everything... at least not at the same time. So think of your priorities not in terms of what activities you do, but when you do them. Timing is everything.

— *Dan Milman*

////////

If you don't design your own life plan, chances are you'll fall into someone else's plan. And guess what they have planned for you? Not much.

— *Jim Rohn*

We aim above the mark to meet the mark.

— Ralph Waldo Emerson

//////////

You need to overcome the tug of people against you as you reach for higher goals.

— George S. Patten

//////////

You must expect great things of yourself before you can do them.

— Michael Jordan

The harder the conflict, the more glorious the truth.

— Thomas Paine

///////////

The wise does at once what the fool does at last.

— Baltasar Gracian

///////////

To begin, begin. — William Wordsworth
The road to success and the road to failure are almost exactly the same.

— Colin R. Davis

Small deeds done are better than great deeds planned.

— Peter Marshall

////////

Motivation will almost always beat mere talent.

— Norman Ralph Augustine

////////

Whatever you want in life, other people are going to want it too. Believe in yourself enough to accept the idea that you have an equal right to it.

— Diane Sawyer

The first step toward success is taken when you refuse to be a captive of the environment in which you first find yourself.

— *Mark Caine*

////////

The hardships that I encountered in the past will help me succeed in the future.

— *Philip Emeagwali*

////////

It's always too early to quit.

— *Norman Vincent Peale*

Perseverance is failing 19 times and succeeding the 20th.

— Julie Andrews

////////////

You can never quit. Winners never quit, and quitters never win.

— Ted Turner

////////////

Arriving at one goal is the starting point to another.

— John Dewey

I'd rather attempt to do something great and fail than to attempt to do nothing and succeed.

— *Robert H. Schuller*

////////

To be successful you must accept all challenges that come your way. You can't just accept the ones you like.

— *Mike Gafka*

////////

Change your thoughts and you change your world.

— *Norman Vincent Peale*

Don't give up. Don't lose hope. Don't sell out.

— Christopher Reeve

////////////

It is very important to know who you are. To make decisions. To show who you are.

— Malala Yousafzai

////////////

Know or listen to those who know.

— Baltasar Gracian

To know oneself, one should assert oneself.

— *Albert Camus*

///////////

If you ask me what I came into this life to do, I will tell you: I came to live out loud.

— *Emile Zola*

///////////

One way to keep momentum going is to have constantly greater goals.

— *Michael Korda*

Change your life today. Don't gamble on the future, act now, without delay.

— *Simon de Beauvoir*

////////

Press forward. Do not stop, do not linger in your journey, but strive for the mark set before you.

— *George Whitefield*

////////

The most effective way to do it, is to do it.

— *Amelia Earhart*

The ultimate aim of the ego is not to see something, but to be something.

— Muhammad Iqbal

////////

How do you know you're going to do something, until you do it?

— J. D. Salinger

////////

Step by step and the thing is done.

— Charles Atlas

Do not weep; do not wax indignant.
Understand.

— *Baruch Spinoza*

///////////

If you've got a talent, protect it.

— *Jim Carrey*

///////////

The key to success is to keep growing in all areas of life: mental, emotional, spiritual, as well as physical.

— *Julius Erving*

Even if you fall on your face, you are still moving forward.

— *Victor Kiam*

////////

Every exit is an entry somewhere else.

— *Tom Stoppard*

////////

Do something wonderful, people may imitate it.

— *Albert Schweitzer*

If you think you can do it, you can.

— *John Burroughs*

////////

Go for it now. The future is promised to no one.

— *Wayne Dyer*

////////

Do not wait to strike till the iron is hot; but make it hot by striking.

— *William Butler Yeats*

What we do today, right now, will have an accumulated effect on all our tomorrows.

— *Alexandra Stoddard*

///////////

Follow your inner moonlight; don't hide the madness.

— *Allen Ginsberg*

///////////

I am not afraid. I was born to do this.

— *Joan of Arc*

The will to succeed is important, but what's more important is the will to prepare.

— Bobby Knight

///////////

Learning is the beginning of wealth.
Learning is the beginning of health.
Learning is the beginning of spirituality.
Searching and learning is where the miracle process all begins.

— Jim Rohn

///////////

Thinking: the talking of the soul with itself.

— Plato

It is in your moments of decision that your destiny is shaped.

— *Tony Robbins*

///////////

To be wholly devoted to some intellectual exercise is to have succeeded in life.

— *Robert Louis Stevenson*

///////////

You never know what motivates you.

— *Cicely Tyson*

Believe you can and you're halfway there.

— *Theodore Roosevelt*

///////////

If opportunity doesn't knock, build a door.

— *Milton Berle*

///////////

Poverty was the biggest motivating factor in my life.

— *Jimmy Dean*

Do not wait for leaders; do it alone, person to person. Be faithful in small things because it is in them that your strength lies.

— *Mother Teresa*

////////

Strong people don't put others down, they lift them up.

— *Michael P. Watson*

Many of life's failures are experienced by people who did not realize how close they were to success when they gave up.

— *Thomas Edison*

//////////

No matter what people tell you, words and ideas can change the world.

— *Robin Williams*

//////////

Begin to be now what you will be hereafter.

— *William James*

There is always room at the top.

— *Daniel Webster*

///////////

Do the difficult things while they are easy and do the great things while they are small. A journey of a thousand miles must begin with a single step.

— *Lao Tzu*

///////////

We should not give up and we should now allow the problem to defeat us.

— *A. P. J. Abdul Kalam*

Try not to become a man of success, but rather try to become a man of value.

— *Albert Einstein*

////////

Look up at the stars and not down at your feet. Try to make sense of what you see, and wonder about what makes the universe exist. Be curious.

— *Stephen Hawking*

////////

The distance between insanity and genius is measured only by success.

— *Bruce Feirstein*

There is only one corner of the universe you can be certain of improving, and that's your own self.

— *Aldous Huxley*

///////////

I don't believe you have to be better than everybody else. I believe you have to be better than you ever thought you could be.

— *Ken Venturi*

///////////

Accept the challenges so you can feel the exhilaration of victory.

— *George S. Patton*

Failure is the opportunity to begin again more intelligently.

— *Henry Ford*

///////////

Don't let the noise of other people's opinions drown out your inner voice.

— *Steve Jobs*

///////////

Aim for success, not perfection. Never give up your right to be wrong, because then you will lose the ability to learn new things and move forward with your life.

— *Dr David M. Burns*

Hard work spotlights the character of people: some turn up their sleeves, some turn up their noses, and some don't turn up at all.

— Sam Ewing

////////

Great people do things before they're ready. They do things before they know they can do it.

— Amy Poehler

////////

People inspire you or they drain you. Pick them wisely.

— Hans F. Hansen

I don't believe in age. I believe in energy. Don't let age dictate what you can and cannot do.

— *Tao Porchon-Lynch*

////////

Failure is the condiment that gives success its flavor.

— *Truman Capote*

////////

The will to win, the desire to succeed, the urge to reach your full potential... these are the keys that will unlock the door to personal excellence.

— *Confucius*

The person who says it cannot be done should not interrupt the person who is doing it.

— *Chinese proverb*

////////

If you judge people you have not time to love them.

— *Mother Teresa*

////////

I can't understand why people are frightened of new ideas. I'm frightened of the old ones.

— *John Cage*

You've got to be willing to lose everything to gain yourself.

— *Iyanla Vanzant*

//////////

Choose people who lift you up.

— *Michelle Obama*

//////////

You've got to get up every morning with determination if you're going to go to bed with satisfaction.

— *George Lorimer*

Done is better than perfect.

— *Sheryl Sandberg*

////////

When something is important enough, you do it even if the odds aren't in your favor.

— *Elon Musk*

////////

By doing what you'd do if you were exactly the person you'd like to be, you'll ultimately become that person.

— *Brian Tracy*

Everyone must choose one of two pains: the pain of discipline or the pain of regret.

— Jim Rohn

////////////

Hard work beats talent when talent doesn't work.

— Unknown

////////////

Making the simple complicated is commonplace; making the complicated simple, awesomely simple, that's creativity.

— Charles Mingus

Success does not consist in never making mistakes but in never making the same one a second time.

— *George Bernard Shaw*

///////////

Collaborate with people you can learn from.

— *Pharrell*

///////////

Success is liking what you do, and liking how you do it.

— *Maya Angelou*

Worrying is like praying for something that you don't want to happen.

— Robert Downey Jr.

////////////

There are two ways of spreading light: to be the candle or the mirror that reflects it.

— Edith Wharton

////////////

Determine never to be idle. No person will have occasion to complain of the want of time who never loses any. It is wonderful how much may be done if we are always doing.

— Thomas Jefferson

Never bend your head. Always hold it high.
Look the world straight in the eye.

— Helen Keller

///////

What kept me sane was knowing that
things would change, and it was a question
of keeping myself together until it did.

— Nina Simone

///////

Falling down is how we grow. Staying down
is how we die.

— Brian Vaszily

Everyone is gifted, but most people never open their package.

— Unknown

////////

They cannot take away our self-respect if we do not give it to them.

— Gandhi

////////

Efforts and courage are not enough without purpose and direction.

— John F. Kennedy

A man can be as great as he wants to be. If you believe in yourself and have the courage, the determination, the dedication, the competitive drive and if you are willing to sacrifice the little things in life and pay the price for the things that are worthwhile, it can be done.

— *Vince Lombardi*

////////////

I can, therefore I am.

— *Simone Weil*

We delight in the beauty of the butterfly, but rarely admit the changes it has gone through to achieve that beauty.

— *Maya Angelou*

///////////

Be who you are and say what you feel, because those who mind don't matter and those who matter don't mind.

— *Dr Seuss*

///////////

You can determine how confident people are by listening to what they don't say about themselves.

— *Brian G. Jett*

Ships in harbour are safe, but that's not what ships are built for.

— John Shedd

////////

What lies beyond us and what lies before us are tiny matters compared to what lies within us.

— Ralph Waldo Emerson

////////

We can't help everyone, but everyone can help someone.

— Ronald Reagan

The greatest discovery of all time is that a person can change his future by merely changing his attitude.

— *Oprah Winfrey*

///////////

Success is the only motivational factor that a boy with character needs.

— *Woody Hayes*

///////////

Happiness is not something you postpone for the future; it is something that you design for the present.

— *Jim Rohn*

Do whatever you do intensely.

— *Robert Henri*

////////////

A will finds a way.

— *Orison Swett Marden*

////////////

Only I can change my life. No one can do it for me.

— *Carol Burnett*

Optimism is the faith that leads to achievement. Nothing can be done without hope and confidence.

— *Helen Keller*

///////////

True happiness involves the full use of one's power and talents.

— *John W. Gardner*

///////////

Quality is not an act, it is a habit.

— *Aristotle*

Good, better, best. Never let it rest. 'Til your good is better and your better is best.

— St. Jerome

////////

Be kind whenever possible. It is always possible.

— Dalai Lama

////////

Always do your best. What you plant now you will harvest later.

— Og Mandino

With the new day comes new strength and new thoughts.

— *Eleanor Roosevelt*

///////////

History will be kind to me, for I intend to write it.

— *Winston Churchill*

///////////

There is nothing deep down inside us except what we have put there ourselves.

— *Richard Rorty*

Thousands of candles can be lighted from a single candle, and the life of the candle will not be shortened. Happiness never decreases by being shared.

— Buddha

///////////

No act of kindness, no matter how small, is ever wasted.

— Aesop

///////////

Someone is sitting in the shade today because someone planted a tree a long time ago.

— Warren Buffett

I hated every minute of training, but I said, 'Don't quit. Suffer now and live the rest of your life as a champion.'

— *Muhammad Ali*

////////

We know what we are, but know not what we may be.

— *William Shakespeare*

////////

The true sign of intelligence is not knowledge but imagination.

— *Albert Einstein*

All speaking is public whether it's to one person or a thousand.

— Roger Love

///////////

A smile is the universal welcome.

— Max Eastman

///////////

A journey of a thousand miles starts with a single step.

— Confucius

Let the world know why you're here and do it with passion.

— Dr Wayne Dyer

////////

I destroy my enemy when I make them my friend.

— Abraham Lincoln

////////

Have the courage to follow your heart and intuition. They somehow know what you truly want to become.

— Steve Jobs

There is no passion to be found playing small — in settling for a life that is less than the one you are capable of living.

— *Nelson Mandela*

//////////

There are two types of people who will tell you that you cannot make a difference in this world: those who are afraid to try and those who are afraid you will succeed.

— *Ray Goforth*

You are a potential genius; there is no problem you cannot solve, and no answer you cannot find somewhere.

— *Brian Tracy*

///////////

Complaining about a problem without posing a solution is called whining.

— *Teddy Roosevelt*

///////////

Failure will never overtake me if my determination to succeed is strong enough.

— *Og Mandino*

You will never win if you never begin.

— Helen Rowland

////////

Life is 10% what happens to you and 90% how you react.

— Charles R. Swindoll

////////

Never give up on something that you can't go a day without thinking about.

— Unknown

If you want to be rich, don't allow yourself the luxury of excuses.

— Robert Kiyosaki

//////////

If not us, who? If not now, when?

— John F. Kennedy

//////////

Other people are going to find healing your wounds. Your greatest life message and your most effective ministry will come out of your deepest hurts.

— Rick Warren

Do what you have to do until you can do what you want to do.

— *Oprah Winfrey*

///////////

Average people talk about people. Exceptional people discuss their dreams.

— *Robin Sharma*

///////////

Nothing is impossible. The word itself says: 'I'm possible'!

— *Audrey Hepburn*

Sometimes your joy is the source of your smile, but sometimes your smile can be the source of your joy.

— *Thich Nhat Hanh*

////////

Your life is your message to the world. Make sure it's inspiring.

— *Les Brown*

////////

It does not matter how slowly you go as long as you don't stop.

— *Confucious*

The path to success is to take massive determined action.

— *Anthony Robbins*

////////

Sometimes the people around you won't understand your journey. They don't need to, it's not for them.

— *Joubert Botha*

////////

You can't change how people treat you or what they say about you. All you can do is change how you react to it.

— *Mohandas Karamchand Gandhi*

Associate yourself with people of good quality, for it is better to be alone than in bad company.

— Booker T. Washington

////////////

If your dreams don't scare you, they are too small.

— Richard Branson

////////////

The best way to predict the future is to create it.

— Abraham Lincoln

The more you inspire the more people will inspire you.

— Simon Sinek

///////////

If you are working on something exciting that you really care about, you don't have to be pushed. The vision pulls you.

— Steve Jobs

///////////

We are what we repeatedly do. Excellence, therefore, is not an act but a habit.

— Aristotle

Do not wait; the time will never be 'just right'. Start where you stand, and work with whatever tools you may have at your command, and better tools will be found as you go along.

— George Herbert

////////////

The reason most people never reach their goals is that they don't define them, or ever seriously consider them as believable or achievable. Winners can tell you where they are going, what they plan to do along the way, and who will be sharing the adventure with them.

— Denis Watiley

Stay hungry. Stay foolish.

— Steve Jobs

//////////

Kind words are short and easy to speak, but their echoes are truly endless.

— Mother Teresa

//////////

Start where you are. Use what you have. Do what you can.

— Arthur Ashe

What is called genius is the abundance of life and health.

— *Henry David Thoreau*

////////////

Creativity is contagious. Pass it on.

— *Albert Einstein*

////////////

The future depends on what we do in the present.

— *Mahatma Gandhi*

Success is a lousy teacher. It seduces smart people into thinking they can't lose.

— *Bill Gates*

////////

Do not pray for an easy life, pray for the strength to endure a difficult one.

— *Bruce Lee*

////////

I CAN is 100 times more important than IQ.

— *Unknown*

Be the change you want to see in the world.

– *Mahatma Gandhi*

////////////

It isn't the mountains ahead to climb that wear you down. It's the pebble in your shoe.

– *Muhammad Ali*

////////////

You have to make it happen.

– *Denis Diderot*

If people are not laughing at your goals, your goals are too small.

— *Azim Premji*

///////

Darkness cannot drive out darkness: only light can do that. Hate cannot drive out hate: only love can do that.

— *Martin Luther King Jr.*

///////

Success is walking from failure to failure with no loss of enthusiasm.

— *Winston Churchill*

When you're curious you find lots of interesting things to do.

— *Walt Disney*

//////////

The truth is, everyone is going to hurt you. You've just got to find the ones worth suffering for.

— *Bob Marley*

//////////

And those who were seen dancing were thought to be insane by those who could not hear the music.

— *Friedrich Nietzsche*

Originality is nothing but judicious
imitation.

— *Voltaire*

///////////

The measure of intelligence is the ability to
change.

— *Albert Einstein*

///////////

Rudeness is the weak man's imitation of
strength.

— *Eric Hoffer*

Your past is just a story. And once you realize this it has no power over you.

— *Chuck Palahniuk*

////////

People who succeed have momentum. The more they succeed, the more they want to succeed, and the more they find a way to succeed. Similarly, when someone is failing, the tendency is to get on a downward spiral that can even become a self-fulfilling prophecy.

— *Tony Robbins*

You create your opportunities by asking for them.

— *Shakti Gawain*

//////////

Imagination is the beginning of creation. You imagine what you desire, you will what you imagine, and at last, you create what you will.

— *George Bernard Shaw*

//////////

Freedom is not worth having if it does not include the freedom to make mistakes.

— *Mahatma Gandhi*

Don't raise your voice, improve your argument.

— *Anonymous*

/////////

Why should you continue going after your dreams? Because seeing the look on the faces of people who said you couldn't... will be priceless.

— *Kevin Ngo*

/////////

Your heaviest artillery will be your will to live. Keep that big gun going.

— *Norman Cousins*

The dog that trots about finds a bone.

— *Golda Meir*

////////

If you want to tell people the truth, make them laugh, otherwise they'll kill you.

— *Oscar Wilde*

////////

Never apologize for having high standards. People who really want to be in your life will rise up to meet them.

— *Unknown*

I am not a has-been. I am a will be.

— Lauren Bacall

////////

Sometimes you don't realize your own strength until you come face to face with your greatest weakness.

— Susan Gale

////////

Keep your face always toward the sunshine — and shadows will fall behind you.

— Walt Whitman

When I dare to be powerful - to use my strength in the service of my vision, then it becomes less and less important whether I am afraid.

— Audre Lorde

////////

Clouds come floating into my life, no longer to carry rain or usher storm, but to add color to my sunset sky.

— Rabindranath Tagore

The greatest glory in living lies not in never falling, but in rising every time we fall.

— *Nelson Mandela*

////////

Things work out best for those who make the best of how things work out.

— *John Wooden*

////////

Whoever is trying to bring you down is already below you.

— *Unknown*

I am grateful for all those difficult people in my life. They have shown me exactly who I don't want to be.

— Unknown

////////

What seems to us as bitter trials are often blessings in disguise.

— Oscar Wilde

////////

What you get by achieving your goals is not as important as what you become by achieving your goals.

— Zig Ziglar

A man ought to do what he thinks is right.

— John Wayne

///////////

A tree falls the way it leans. Be careful which way you lean.

— The Lorax

///////////

Amateurs sit and wait for inspiration, the rest of us just get up and go to work.

— Stephen King

If you're born poor it's not your mistake. If you die poor, it's your mistake.

— Bill Gates

////////

I don't want to get to the end of my life and find that I lived just the length of it. I want to have lived the width of it as well.

— Diane Ackerman

////////

Tough times never last, but tough people do.

— Dr Robert Schuller

Sometimes adversity is what you need to face in order to become successful.

— *Zig Ziglar*

///////////

Whenever you see a successful person you only see the public glories, never the private sacrifices to reach them.

— *Vaibhav Shah*

///////////

It is the mark of an educated mind to be able to entertain a thought without accepting it.

— *Aristotle*

We are all broken. That is how the light gets in.

— *Ernest Hemingway*

/////////

Nobody can hurt me without my permission.

— *Gandhi*

/////////

Life is tough, my darling, but so are you.

— *Stephanie Bennett-Henry*

Wake up with determination, go to bed with satisfaction.

— *Unknown*

///////////

It's not what you achieve, it's what you overcome. That's what defines your career.

— *Carlton Fisk*

///////////

If you want to achieve greatness, stop asking for permission.

— *Anonymous*

The difference between ordinary and extraordinary is that little extra.

— Jimmy Johnson

////////

Deserve your dream.

— Octavio Paz

////////

Everyone morning you have two choices: continue to sleep with your dreams or get up and chase them.

— Unknown

Today you are you that is truer than true.
There is no one alive who is more youer than
you.

— Dr Seuss

////////////

Don't waste words on people who deserve
your silence. Sometimes the most powerful
thing you can say is nothing at all.

— Mandy Hale

////////////

Be somebody who makes everybody feel
like a somebody.

— Unknown

It's about being alive and feisty and not
sitting down and shutting up even though
people would like you to.

— Pink

//////////

I had no idea what history was being made,
I was just tired of giving up.

— Rosa Parks

//////////

There is no chance, no destiny, no fate, that
can hinder or control the firm resolve of a
determined soul.

— Ella Wheeler Wilcox

If you want to make everyone happy, don't be a leader — sell ice-cream.

— Steve Jobs

///////////

They key is to keep company only with people who uplift you, whose presence calls forth your best.

— Epictetus

///////////

A somebody was once a nobody who wanted to and did.

— John Burroughs

Integrity is doing the right thing, even when no-one is watching.

— *C.S. Lewis*

////////

Praise is a wonderful people-builder. Catch individuals doing something right.

— *Brian Tracy*

////////

Big shots are just little shots who keep shooting.

— *Christopher Morley*

Weak people revenge. Strong people forgive. Intelligent people ignore.

— *Unknown*

////////

A lot of people are afraid to say what they want. That's why they don't get what they want.

— *Madonna*

////////

Here is the simple but powerful rule... always give people more than they expect to get.

— *Nelson Boswell*

Be the person your dog thinks you are.

— *JW Stephens*

////////

Dream big, smart small, act now.

— *Robin Sharma*

////////

If you want to make a permanent change, stop focusing on the size of your problems and start focusing on the size of you!

— *T. Harv Eker*

Don't worry so much about knowing the right people. Just make yourself worth knowing.

— *Scott Hurtado*

////////

Be miserable. Or motivate yourself. Whatever has to be done, it's always your choice.

— *Wayne Dyer*

////////

What sunshine is to flowers, smiles are to humanity.

— *Joseph Addison*

Do you want to know who you are? Don't ask. Act! Action will delineate and define you.

— Thomas Jefferson

////////

You must take action now that will move you towards your goals. Develop a sense of urgency in your life.

— H. Jackson Brown, Jr.

////////

People buy into the leader before the vision.

— John Maxwell

Unexpected kindness is the most powerful, least costly, and most underrated agent of human change.

— *Bob Kerrey*

////////

If you hear a voice inside you say 'you cannot paint', by all means paint, and that voice will be silenced.

— *Vincent Van Gogh*

////////

Failure defeats losers, failure inspires winners.

— *Robert T. Kiyosaki*

Minds are like parachutes, they only function when they are open.

— *James Dewar*

////////////

I can't change the direction of the wind, but I can adjust my sails to always reach my destination.

— *Jimmy Dean*

////////////

Genius is 1% inspiration and 99% perspiration.

— *Thomas Edison*

Act as if what you do makes a difference. It does.

— *William James*

///////////

October is about trees revealing colors they've hidden all year. People have an October as well.

— *Jim Storm*

///////////

Leaders who don't listen will eventually be surrounded by people who have nothing to say.

— *Andy Stanley*

I know not age, nor weariness nor defeat.

— Rose Kennedy

//////////

Who seeks shall find.

— Sophocies

//////////

A good plan violently executed now is better than a perfect plan executed next week.

— George S. Patten

Happiness lies in the joy of achievement, in the thrill of creative effort.

— *Franklin D. Roosevelt*

//////////

If you are not willing to risk the usual, you will have to settle for the ordinary.

— *Jim Rohn*

//////////

Challenges are what make life interesting; overcoming them is what makes life meaningful.

— *Unknown*

He conquers who endures.

— *Persius*

////////

Have the confidence to reach for your dreams, and believe that you can be successful.

— *Rex Maughan*

////////

I've always tried to be a step past wherever people expected me to be.

— *Beverly Sills*

Fear of failure, it's the greatest motivational tool. It drives me and drives me and drives me.

— *Jerry West*

////////

I come to win.

— *Leo Durocher*

////////

Develop success from failures. Discouragement and failure are two of the surest stepping stones to success.

— *Dale Carnegie*

One may miss the mark by aiming too high as too low.

— *Thomas Fuller*

////////

No one is perfect. That is why pencils have erasers.

— *Unknown*

////////

Our prime purpose in life is to help others.

— *Dalai Lama*

I think it's possible for ordinary people to choose to be extraordinary.

— Elon Musk

///////////

Freedom is nothing but a chance to be better.

— Albert Camus

///////////

Reading is the mind what exercise is to the body.

— Sir Richard Steele

Stop stopping yourself.

— Unknown

////////////

Before you put on a frown, make absolutely sure there are no smiles available.

— Jim Beggs

////////////

Coca-Cola sold only 25 bottles in its first year. Never give up.

— Unknown

Your energy introduces you before you even speak.

— *Unknown*

///////////

Be as you wish to seem.

— *Socrates*

///////////

The weeds keep multiplying in our garden, which is our mind ruled by fear. Rip them out and call them by name.

— *Sylvia Browne*

Life isn't about waiting for the storm to pass. It's about learning how to dance in the rain.

— *Vivian Greene*

//////////

The pessimist complains about the wind. The optimist expects it to change. The leader adjusts the sales.

— *John Maxwell*

//////////

Discipline is doing what you hate to do but nonetheless doing it like you love it.

— *Mike Tyson*

You are not here merely to make a living.
You are here in order to enable the world
to live more amply, with greater vision,
with a finer spirit of hope and achievement.
You are here to enrich the world, and
you impoverish yourself if you forget the
errand.

— *Woodrow Wilson*

////////////

If you want to conquer fear, don't sit home
and think about it. Go out and get busy.

— *Dale Carnegie*

Don't be afraid to give up the good to go for the great.

— *John D. Rockefeller*

////////

No masterpiece was ever created by a lazy artist.

— *Anonymous*

////////

Happiness is a butterfly, which when pursued, is always beyond your grasp, but which, if you will sit down quietly, may alight upon you.

— *Nathaniel Hawthorne*

Blessed are those who can give without remembering and take without forgetting.

— Anonymous

///////////

What's the point of being alive if you don't at least try to do something remarkable.

— Anonymous

///////////

Life is not about finding yourself. Life is about creating yourself.

— Lolly Daskal

Nothing in the world is more common than unsuccessful people with talent.

— *Anonymous*

////////

Knowledge is being aware of what you can do. Wisdom is knowing when not to do it.

— *Anonymous*

////////

Your problem isn't the problem. Your reaction is the problem.

— *Anonymous*

The starting point of all achievement is desire.

— Napolean Hill

///////

Success is the sum of small efforts, repeated day-in and day-out.

— Robert Collier

///////

If you want to achieve excellence, you can get there today. As of this second, quit doing less-than-excellent work.

— Thomas J. Watson

We become what we think about most of the time, and that's the strangest secret.

— Earl Nightingale

//////////

The only place where success comes before work is in the dictionary.

— Vidal Sassoon

//////////

I find that when you have a real interest in life and a curious life, that sleep is not the most important thing.

— Martha Stewart

It's not what you look at that matters, it's what you see.

— *Anonymous*

////////

A real entrepreneur is somebody who has no safety net underneath them.

— *Henry Kravis*

////////

Most of the important things in the world have been accomplished by people who have kept on trying when there seemed to be no help at all.

— *Dale Carnegie*

I hope you enjoyed these
quotes, and would love to
hear about your favorite
ones in a review
on Amazon.

• • • • •

Please check out our
other books for even more
motivation and inspiration.

Made in the USA
Columbia, SC
02 April 2020